Marry Me With

Marigolds

Selected Poems
1998 to 2013

Sylvia Berek Rosenthal

Cover art & design by Elaine Grab
Book design by Donna Van Sant

Marry Me with Marigolds
Copyright © 2015 by Sylvia Berek Rosenthal
First Edition, April 2015

ISBN: 978-0-9883006-6-8
LOCCN: 2015938395

Designed and printed in USA by
dvs publishing
2824 Winthrop Avenue
San Ramon, CA 94583

This book of poetry is dedicated to

Diane Capito

Who was the most giving person I have ever met.
She was also the very best friend I have ever had.
There are several other people who claim
that Diane was the very best friend they ever had.

Each of them speaks the absolute truth.

Diane Capito
May 20, 1931 to June 27, 2009

Beloved Friend
Artist
Beloved Friend
Writer
Beloved Friend

oh how
we
miss you

Contents

A Few of My Favorites

Food and Family

This and That and Much Such Important Stuff

Love and Loss

Introduction

It's not my fault.

It was an accident. Not even my accident. My late husband, George's accident. He took a really bad fall and shattered his shoulder. Sirens, medics, ambulance and what seemed like an endless drive to the hospital. And I followed the ambulance to the hospital in the dark. I never drive in the dark. I don't really see well enough to do that. And it was two days before Christmas and the only surgeon we knew was on vacation.

Eventually our surgeon came home. He replaced George's shattered shoulder with a spanking new bionic one. Told me to bring George home and take very good care of him for the next six weeks. It would take that long for George's body and his new shoulder to decide if they liked each other enough to stay together for forever.

The world's greatest 24 hour a day caretaker is not me and after just a few days, I began hunting for an excuse to get away. As soon as George could answer a telephone and get to the bathroom by himself off I went.

I had been writing personal essays for years, so I headed to the San Antonio branch of Texas University to look for a writing course to improve my skills. The only two writing classes available were "How to Write Business Letters" and "Writing Poetry".

I'd never written any poetry but I certainly wasn't going to take a course on writing business letters.

"Writing Poetry" was an undergraduate course taught by a young and stimulating instructor. The students were welcoming and just as inspiring. This was the most exciting adventure I'd had in forever. I probably worked an eight hour day during that entire time and loved most of it.

I've been writing poetry, reading poetry, and taking classes in poetry ever since. It started in San Antonio, continued in San Miguel de Allende, and still goes on in the Bay Area of California. You are about to read some of it right now.

But remember....

It's not my fault.

Acknowledgements

Best Friends appeared in Voices along the River 2002
How Come appeared in Voices along the River 2003
For Jenny Joseph won the poetry contest of the American
Society on Aging and appeared in Atencion
Hill Country after the Rain appeared in the San Antonio
Express News
Hummingbird appeared in El Independente
Alter Berek is Old, *Chopped Liver* and *The Suit* all appeared
in Poetica Magazine
Marry Me with Marigolds won the 2010 Benicia, Ca, Poets
Love Poem Contest

Nightgowns Don't Work has been the favorite poem of poets
I worked with in San Antonio, Texas; San Miguel de Allende,
Mexico; and Clayton and Concord, California. It has also
been the favorite of audiences at all of my poetry readings in
all three places.

Nightgowns Don't Work has never been offered for
publication anywhere; nor has it ever been entered in any
contest.

I hereby bequeath it to all those who have ever enjoyed it.

Thank You

For every poetry book I've ever read and for every poet I have heard read.
To every poetry teacher I've ever had.
For every poetry lecture I've attended.
To every student in each poetry class I've ever taken.
For every poetry workshop I've attended.

There was always something to learn from each and every one of them.
And I learned.
And I learned.

And A Very Special Thank You

To Elaine Grab for taking her beautiful photograph and using it so skillfully to create the cover for this book

To Donna Van Sant, my editor and technical wizard, who shepherded me through this process, showed how lots more work and lots more care could make it better and then put it all together.

Thank you   Thank you Thank you

A
Few
of My
Favorites

How Come

Whenever I'm on the phone
    He really becomes hungry and wants to know what's for dinner—
    even if we just ate.

Or

    He can't find that most important piece of paper. It was right
    there on the desk. I must have moved it. He would never have
    misplaced it. Of course eventually it mysteriously, magically
    reappears between the other two sheets he's holding in his hand.

Or

    He comes in smiling, unfolding the half full crinkly crackly bag of
    potato chips and finishes eating them crunch by noisy crunch.

Or

    Now is the time to fix the cabinet door that's been sticking for the
    past two years. He's been meaning to fix it for the past two years.
    It only takes a tap here, a whack there, a veritable cacophony of
    boffs and bangs. I can't hear a thing, but now that cabinet door
    doesn't stick—quite as much.

If all else fails

He comes up behind me, nibbles my ear, nuzzles the back of my neck,
slides his hand into my blouse

****

I   hang   up.!

Marry Me With Marigolds

Marry me with marigolds
Tempt me with your tenderness
Covet me with coriander
Chocolate and
Cloves

Favor me with foxglove
Gather me the garden's garland
Circle me with summer squash
Sesame and
Sage

Woo me with water lilies
Nurture me with nutmeg
Pamper me with peppers
Red green and
Gold

And I will stroke
Your balding head
Bake you babkas
Cook you cabbages
Pat your pot belly

If you will only
Marry me with marigolds

Condolences

Don't believe them
When they say
It will get easier
It won't get easier
You will learn
To live with the loss
To live with the loneliness
And you must begin
To get on
With your life
There is no viable
Alternative

From one
Who has been there
Who is there

Maid in America

My mother was born in Detroit
You can't get any more American than that
Can You?

When she turned seventeen
She met my father.
He spoke Yiddish and Polish
She spoke only English.
They had no trouble.
Pillow talk worked just fine.
When she turned eighteen
They celebrated by getting married.

One year later
World War One
Began.

What a time in America.
Every true blue American became a patriot.
Every non-citizen became an alien
Every alien became an enemy.
People marched
Congress acted.
"All aliens must register
Any woman who marries
An alien loses her citizenship."
Could they do that
Could they say you weren't born
Where you were born
Could they make you disappear?

Not Rosie
Not my mother!
She stood up and yelled
"No way fellas
Look I'm here
Here I am."

When Papa
Applied
For citizenship
Mama did too.

Official number one asked Rosie where she was born.
"Detroit'" she said.
"Harrumph" said official number one.

Official number two asked, "Where were your parents born?"
"Hungary," said Rosie.
"Harrumph," said official number two.

Official number three asked my father, "Where were you born?"
Papa said, "I was born in Russia, but now it's Poland"
"Harrumph," said official number three.

Officials 1, 2, and 3 put their heads together.
They were perturbed and they pondered.
After due deliberation
They decided.

To Rosie
They said

"You are Russian, Polish, Hungarian, American
Here are your papers.
We hereby declare you a
Naturalized citizen of these United States.

Someday you may vote
But you can never become
President."

Nightgowns Don't Work

No matter what kind you buy
Nightgowns don't work.
Buy the straight, sedate, ladylike kind
It looks just lovely when you put it on.
Flop into bed, curl up on your side
And your knee tries to poke its way through the fabric.
Pull it up to find some comfort
And your toenail gets caught in the hem.
OUCH!
They just don't work.

Buy a "baby doll" gown
And you'll be comfortable.
It's short and wide
Like a little girl's pinafore.
But what big girl wants to be
Caught dead in a "baby doll".

Buy a nice roomy flannel granny gown.
Now that has space aplenty
For knees and toes and sundry other parts.
Flop into bed, curl up on your side
And it feels just fine.

Wiggle a little, turn over, or try to
And the flannel gown stays glued to the sheet.
Tug, pull, yank, then tug some more

You finally get that flannel to come along.
But now it's in lumps and bumps
That plague your belly and assault your thighs.
Nightgowns just don't work.

Then there's that special occasion nightgown
The one that costs half a month's salary
The one that's Victoria's Secret.
It weighs ten grams and hides nothing
You spend the rent money without a qualm
You know what you want
You know what you hope for.

Should things work out
By the time that gown gets on
You'll be ready to take it off.
Nightgowns just don't work!

A Cautionary Tale Of The Castle Keep

Forsooth, dear Father Pottbelli, we require not that you perform
        last rites.
We require that you abet a rescue.
My dearly beloved sister and I have been held captive in
        this castle keep
For lo three centuries and more.
The cause we know not. We mean none harm.

Of late our sufferings have grown more acute.

Until four decades past
We had the privilege of all the keep.
Dear Sister Dragonia could cavort and frolic in the glen
With all the babes and pups
But now, with no just cause, Lord Mountbutton confines us
        both.
We may not stray beyond the castle walls.

For myself, I ask no boon.
But, oh, how Dragonia suffers.
The scales of her three tails do dull
And she has not had a babe for breakfast in four long
        decades.

I succor her with all the potions I command
Newt oil brewed in salamander broth
Spaniel eyes baked in musky fen marsh
Yet she remains so pale.
I gather her moonbeams and morning dew
All to no avail.

For my precious sister
I beseech thee
Send a knight in shining armor.
Let him hurry hither on a swift white steed
Approach the castle walls
With muffled tread
And wait in silence beneath the parapet.

We'll wait in silence up on high
When at last brave knight we spy
One last embrace
One last goodbye
Then will Dragonia leap upon him
Clasp his waist with clutching claws
Grasp his throat with gripping jaws
The knight shall howl
The horse shall neigh
And once again
Dragonia shall play!

Rope Bridge

Hands grasp prickly thick braided rope rails
One foot steps onto narrow shaky laced boards
Other foot stays tightly glued to terra firma.
It does not wish to test the boards
That sway endlessly endlessly
In front of us.

Finally other foot takes the plunge
Oh my God—plunge
No not plunge.
Just place one foot in front of the other
And you will move
No need to open your eyes.
It's swaying more and more
As I move further out
The wind is stronger

The sound of the water below is louder.
It feels closer
oh my God
I feel the spray
I have to look
Oh my god
It's not close
It's at least a mile down.

A mile down
To dark churning water
And I'm beginning to feel sick
And the rope is burning my hand
And the backpack is coming loose
And I'm going to whoops
Right here on this thing
They call a bridge
In front of all these people.

Ten more steps
And I'm on real land
But I'm still swaying
It still feels like it's swaying.

Less than five hundred steps
It felt like five million.
Thank God we don't have to do that again
WE DO
HAVE TO DO IT AGAIN

Not today
Please not today.

For Jenny Joseph

You said

     When I am an old woman I shall wear purple.

Well I am an old woman

     I do wear purple, pink, and polka dots

     Lots of polka dots

But more than that.

I don't finish every book I start.

     Sorry mama, you were wrong

I don't HAVE TO finish everything.

     I'll read anything that is fun

     that touches me

     that suddenly tells me something

     I didn't even know I wanted to know.

But writing that is turned in on itself

     so convoluted

     I have to dig and burrow

     to find some meaning.

Oh no!

My time now is flexible

     there are very few "have-to's."

But my time now is valuable

     and I choose to husband it.

I won't stay to the end

     of a lackluster play

     a pointless movie

     a tedious lecture.

It's bad enough the money's gone

I won't also squander my time.

But oh there are compensations
        audition for a part in a play?
                Sure!
        write a story?
        invent a poem?
                But of course!
        climb a mountain?
        swim a lake?
        ford a river?
                If I can dear, if I can!

Now that I am failing
        I can allow myself
        to fail

But I do dare

        And sometimes I succeed!

Home Cookin'

Even before we were married
George told me
The best food in the world
The very best   is
French fries and steak
The way mamma makes it

The loving young bride
Tried to make
French fries and steak
The way mamma makes it

The bride's was OK
Of course we ate it
But it never made the grade
I broke the budget
Buying porterhouse and filet mignon
Tried and tried but it never was
The way mamma makes it

Finally I asked mamma
to let me watch

Early in the morning
She fried the potatoes
Hard crisp and delicious
Dumped them in a bowl
To cool and sog till dinner

Dinnertime
She took round steak
Put it into a hot oily pan
Turned it and pressed it
Cooked it forever

George is right
No matter what
I'll never do
Steak and French fries
The way mamma does it

Ceremony

The truck crawled up the mountain as long as a semblance of a road existed. Then it dumped us out and backed down the mountain. All five of us stood shivering in the early morning foggy cold. Ahead of us stretched a single file overgrown path. We had to follow it for three miles to the top of the mountain, to that special grove of trees where the ceremony would take place. A long cold three mile hike up from an altitude of 10,000 feet to an altitude of 12,000 feet.

I had trouble breathing even before we started to move. I felt light headed and somewhat disoriented. Then we began hiking. With each step we crunched over desiccated cadavers. We had no choice. This was the only way to get there. And getting there took a long hard time. We stopped to catch our breath, to rest our bodies, to wonder if this was worth all the effort. We felt as though we had been hiking for an eternity, but it was still before noon when we reached the grove.

There we were in the middle of a forest of tall strange trees, whose forbears had been pushed to these mountaintops way back during the ice age. Each tree had many big black clumps on both their trunks and branches. Clumps as big as giant melons, but these clumps were not smooth, and they seemed to shift in size and shape as we looked at them.

The clumps were the center and the essence of the ceremony we had come for. And now all we could do was wait. If the fog did not lift, there would be nothing. Likewise if the sun failed to emerge brightly, there would be no ceremony. All we could do was stand there and wait.

The fog began to lift, and the clumps began expanding and shifting shape. Then the sun began burning off the rest of the fog, and shined more and more brightly.

Magically the clumps exploded into hundreds of thousands of brilliant black, white and orange Monarch butterflies. We were surrounded, enveloped, incorporated into this ever changing cycle of light, color and movement. The dull clumps reformed and then exploded into color and graceful movement, again, and yet again, and we were embedded in this fantastic yet natural and recurring phenomenon.

Misery

I'm miserable
I sneeze
I cough
I wheeze
I drip

I'm miserable
My head is stuffed
My fever soars
My cheeks are puffed
My nose just pours

I'm miserable
When will I
Be rid of this
Just to breathe again
Instead of hiss

I'm very good. Do just what the doctor orders. Drink two gallons a day. Get lots of bed rest. Can't stand up without listing and grabbing on. Of course I get plenty of bed rest in between bouts and waves of wheezing and coughing and ever increasing levels of fever.

Dear doctor is so sympathetic orders magic of antibiotics. Of course there will be attendant side effects. Whatever still worked, just won't anymore. Yeast infections in any and all mucous membranes are quite common. Your bowels and your belly don't cotton to antibiotics. They'll notice and object. Eat lots of plain yoghurt, that tends to lessen the length and depth of these symptoms.

I moan
And groan
I fuss
And fume
I feel like I'm buried in
This small stale room

I'm miserable
My eyes tear
My ears go pop
My throat is raw
When will it stop

I'm miserable
Drink orange juice
And lots of hot tea
Every five minutes
I have to pee

I'm miserable
What did I do
To deserve this plague
I had a shot for the flu
One for pneumonia too
A lot of good they did
Boo hoo boo hoo

I'm definitely, absolutely, positively,
Thoroughly, unequivocally miserable!!!

Damn

That mealy mouthed sniveling brown-nosing worm of a desk clerk.
It's all his fault.

I had taken care of the mess, I'd cleaned it all up just fine.
Taken the whole bloody mess of clothes and sheets home.
Washed 'em twice with double bleach.
Came back to room. Got rid of him.
Made the bed.
Spent an hour on my knees cleaning the rug....

JoJo is a great husband. He loves the kids.
We go out on the town now and then.
But mostly, he's a homebody.
He loves his telly, and poker
With the same three beer guzzling guys all these years.
He's not been much for the bedroom bounces
Not ever. Really. Not ever.

He don't count pennies.
So I can buy a thing or two on my own.

Do a thing or two on my own, if you know what I mean.
And I get hungry for some nookie.
JoJo is a great husband.
I love him.
But he's zero in that department.

So I've worked it all out.
Pick up a hunk of a bloke in a bar,
A drinking buddy with benefits and no strings.
It almost always works.
Fair exchange. Everybody's happy.

Especially me. Especially JoJo....
Who don't know a thing about it.

Then this guy. He's to blame too.
All of a sudden, for no damn reason, he says he loves me.
What an ass. He's great in the sack
But who the hell wants anything else from him?
And three months is long enough.
Maybe too long.
I can't convince him it's over.
He's going to talk to JoJo
Oh my god would that mess me up.
I talk. I beg. I shake him.

I shake him so hard he bangs into the bedpost.
Again....
And again....
The back of his head mashes into a gooey drippy blob.... and
It's really over.
And I clean it all up. And I'm done. Then,

This damn sniveling desk clerk comes along
With moving pictures!
He had a camera in my room
Making movies of the whole three months,
That's how he got his jollies.
And he even had that last night.
And me scrubbing the rug!
That pervert.
That mealy mouthed desk clerk....

It's all his fault.

Woman with Fans

I've enjoyed *Woman with Fans* in reproductions
Many times.
It's a lively painting to see in reproduction
A charming composition.
The swath of black gown carries you
Round and round inside the entire frame
And stops you—as it should
At the lovely head and smiling face
Of the woman with fans
Flat smooth and gracious
All very pretty.

Then I saw Manet's actual painting.

This wonderful woman with fans
Is stretched out on a couch.
But you can almost feel her eagerness to get up
To get off the couch
To tell the painter
Je ne sais qua.
To tell tales of brightness and color
Color to rival the myriad tones and
Colors of the actual painting.
Layer upon layer of many colors
Many brushstrokes
All create the illusion
Of light coming
Through the canvas
Reflecting back
Illuminating
This wonderful woman with fans.

Food
and
Family

Chanukah

What do we celebrate on Chanukah
We celebrate the *Maccabees*
And we make *latkes*

The Syrians are driven out
The temple is cleansed
And we eat *latkes*

Watch one day's worth of oil
Last for eight long days
And we make *latkes*

Exchange presents all eight days
Give children Chanukah *gelt*
And we eat *latkes*

Spin the *dreidl*
Put and take
And we eat more *latkes*

Gut Yontiff

Nineteen Hundred and Forty Six

His war is over
hearty welcome home for the hero
from me—his wife, his two year old daughter
whom he doesn't even know
his mother and father
all stuck together
in a one bedroom, one bath
three room apartment
hearty welcome home for the hero.

Such closeness, such intimacy
can't draw a solitary breath
always in touch
almost hear each other's thoughts
inside each other's skin
attacked, bombarded, disintegrated
where am I?

Thursday evenings are mine
Ride the subway to Hunter College
leave home early
arrive long before class
take empty elevator to the fifth floor
walk echoing corridor to 523
slide past the door
shut it behind me.

Big empty room
silent student chairs
smooth flat desk
in front of cool
green slate
light—air—space
blessedly alone.

For one glorious
half hour
a whole room
all my own.

The Suit

Thirteen—all grown up
Shop for my clothes—all by myself.
But this time it's special.

Papa says,
"Sylvie, go shop for a suit.
A tailored suit
It should be all wool.
You're big enough for a real ladies' suit
For spring, for *Pesach*, for the *Seders*.
Navy blue or brown or maybe even a pinstripe would be good.
A tailored suit, a dark color it shouldn't show dirt
Something you'll get a lot of wear out of.
Twenty dollars is all you should have to pay for such a suit.
Here's twenty dollars.
Well, if you see just what you want and it's a little more
But twenty five—tops.
Here, ten, twenty, thirty.
You'll bring change
Put it in the inside pocket
Be careful."

Wow
A suit a real suit
And so much money.
I never carried so much money before.
Down into the subway
The Lexington Avenue line
All the way to Fourteenth Street
Union Square.

Not for parades and soap box speeches
But the bargain buyers heaven.
Kleins and Orbachs
New York City's two prime low priced stores.
Mostly just cheap stuff
But thrown in, some throwaways from really good shops.

Kleins I love
Orbachs is a little too toney.
Uptown ladies bargain hunting
Looking funny at a thirteen year old shopping alone.

Straight to the ladies' suits
Only size fourteen.
Don't look if it don't fit.
Not a fancy store
Not everything in every size
So
Don't look if it don't fit.

Lots and lots and lots of suits.
All wool like Papa said.
Navy blue, brown, no pin stripes.
But oh so dull
So ordinary like cousin Millie's
Or cousin Rachel's.
I try one on
It looks all right—just all right.

But then
Oh then
A suit jumps off the rack
And throws itself at me.
A plaid
Powder blue with light coffee lines
Fuzzy soft, baby fuzz
Pleated skirt
Patch pocketed jacket lined in powder blue silk.

I tried it on
And
It was wonderful
Like nothing I had ever worn
Like nothing I had ever seen.
I was the country squire's daughter
The best dressed lady in the Easter Parade
First prize winner in the spelling bee.

But oh my god, what would Papa say
It was the whole thirty dollars.
It wasn't brown or tailored or navy blue.
But it was all wool
I couldn't leave it
But what would Papa say?

Papa said,
"Sylvie, not just the money.
It's just not practical
Sure it looks good on.
It's well made
Handmade buttonholes
Hand felled seams.

But the color's so light, the weave's loose
It'll catch on everything.

It'll always be dirty
It won't last at all.

You'll have it for one season
Such a lot of money for one season.

Come look Sylvie
Sunday I'll take you down to Division Street
To the wholesale houses.
There you get the best
The very best
Even if it's more money.
You'll see
You'll find something you like even better
You'll buy it and you'll love it.

This one here is only a *shmatte* a rag.
Monday you'll take it back to Klein's and believe me
You'll be happy with a good new suit."

We went on Sunday
We trudged through every wholesale house.
I tried on navy blue, brown and even pin stripe.
But nothing would do
Nothing I liked even a little bit.

Mama talked to Papa
Papa talked to Mama.
Finally Papa said,
"Sylvie, you want the plaid one so bad
You should have it.
Enjoy it while it lasts.

Next time you'll buy a good suit."

Alter Berek Is Old

Alter Berek stands not so tall
But oh so proud
Bube Basha's been dead for
Ten long years
Zeyde Alter lives alone
Most of the time
Makes unsatisfactory visits
To each of his children
In turn

He can't live alone any more
The children all agree

Oatmeal put up to cook
And then forgotten
Til the smell of scorch
Brings next door neighbor running

Bath water turned on
And then forgotten
Til downstairs neighbor comes shrieking
"You've flooded my bedroom
Again!"

My father comes to talk with Zeyde
Quietly—sensibly

The Daughters of Jacob Home for the Aged
Is a lovely place
High on a hill
Across from Crotona Park

Alter Berek listens and says nothing

My father tries again
They serve three good meals a day
And you have choices
They have hot tea in glasses
With lump sugar
Every evening
You love tea with lump sugar

Alter Berek listens and says nothing

My father tries some more
You can have your private room and your own bathroom
They take your laundry twice a week
And bring back everything
Clean and pressed

Alter Berek listens and says
"Izzie, you really think it's so good?"
My father answers
"Absolutely, Pop, I think it's really the very best"

Alter Berek listens—ponders a while
Then he says
"Izzie if you think it's so good
You go
Me
I'll stay right where I am"

Bagels Mexico

A world without bagels is like
A world without sunshine
In Mexico
I had *bollillos*
But no bagels
I had *tortillas*
But no bagels
I had *chalupas*
But no bagels

So I made them
I mixed
And I kneaded
I raised
And I punched down
I shaped
And I boiled
I baked
And I cooled

And then
I ate them
I spread them
With cream cheese
And I ate them
I topped them
With tuna
And I ate them
I covered them
With a hill of chopped liver
And I ate them

Oh, yes I ate 'em
I shared them with neighbors
I flung them at friends
I presented them as presents

And oh yes
I ate 'em

Breakfast

Breakfast takes a long time at our house even
When it's just grapefruit and coffee
The breakfast table sits just in front of the big picture window
And what a picture
We face the grassy commons
About half a block wide and one block long
It's the commons but we really think we own it

Just in front of the window is a great big spreading live oak
It was a small tree when we moved in 17 years ago
Now its many branches stretch out in a
Wide sheltering circle

Hanging quite low, so I can reach them, are two seed feeders
George made these special feeders to very rigid specifications
The space between the roof and dish of each feeder
Had to be big enough to invite sparrows, titmice and
Even cardinals to come on in and feast
But the space had to be small enough to discourage doves and
Grackles from trying to take over the whole party

The feeders work just fine
The doves try to get in but never make it
We don't let them go hungry   We toss some seed
On the ground and the sparrows swing enough
Down their way to keep them well fed

Every morning we are treated to a well-choreographed bird ballet
From bush to feeder, from feeder to tree and back again
With gyrating rotating place changes at center stage
Occasionally a ballet star puts in an appearance
And scatters the entire chorus
Last week it was a golden fronted woodpecker that made
A three point landing on the feeder   Its claws on the edge
Its tail underneath the dish   Like a balancing rudder
and its beak pecking away at the food

This morning, the ballet star was a bluebird   The first time ever
A bluebird

Breakfast takes a long time at our house

Chopped Liver

Anyone can make chopped liver
It's just a mix of hard boiled eggs
Chicken liver and onion fried in fat
Seasoned with salt and chopped up

Anyone can ruin it too
Substitute any other kind of liver
Fry in butter
Chop to a fare thee well and
You may have a paté
But for sure
It ain't chopped liver

So you want me to tell you
How to make real chopped liver
Just cause you've eaten mine
And you want more

All right
So I'll tell you
Give me a taste when you make it
Something of it
Is still mine
Even when you make it

First hard boil four eggs
What?
You want to know how to boil eggs
And how to peel them

Just forget it
Go away
If you can't boil and peel an egg
You are not ready

You wouldn't try to
Run the marathon
If you couldn't already
Run a block

Making chopped liver is
High class stuff
You have to be
A comfortable cook first

Go away
Come back when
You at least know
How to boil an egg

Now for those of you
Who know how to boil an egg
Let's continue
Put some oil in the bottom of
A heavy bottomed pan

If you have chicken fat
Use it
Half oil half chicken fat is
Absolutely the best
Oil for smoothness
Chicken fat for flavor

What
Even the cooks are giving me trouble
Too much cholesterol in chicken fat
Listen

If you are even going to
Think about cholesterol
Stop right now
Give up
Don't make chopped liver

Please don't tell me about string beans
No fat salad dressing
Only egg whites
Those things don't make chopped liver
They make rabbit food
Either we make chopped liver
Or we part company

No more foolishness
No more questions
This is hard enough

While the fat is slowly warming
Cube one good sized onion
A yellow onion please
Not red
Not white
Yellow onions only please

Put that onion into the sizzling fat
Let it fry until it becomes half brown
Cube another onion
Throw it into the pan

When that onion is half brown
Throw in a pound of cleaned chicken livers
Fry the whole mess until
The liver is thoroughly cooked

I used to like this even better
When I barely cooked the liver
But salmonella does scare me
So cook it well

Cube one more good sized onion
Throw on a teaspoon of salt
Yes leave that last onion
Raw
And that's all it takes
That's all except for chopping

Now take your grandmother's
Wooden chopping bowl and knife
Use your strong right arm
And chop away
You won't chop too long
Your arm will feel like it's coming off
Before you can chop too long

On the other hand
If you use a food processor
Like most of us
BE CAREFUL

Fill it one third full
Use only short pulses
Stop BEFORE you think
It's chopped enough
IT IS CHOPPED ENOUGH

When you've chopped it all
And mixed it all together
Taste it
It probably needs more salt
So add it

Cover it
Refrigerate it
Go out and buy two loaves of rye bread

Invite your friends
Have a party
You've got real chopped liver

Damn Him

HURL DOWN THE EMBANKMENT
GRAB OARS FROM LOCKER
THROW THEM INTO THE BOAT
SHOVE OFF SHORE
JUMP IN
BANG OARS INTO OARLOCKS
AND ROW

ROW HARDER
ROW FASTER
ROW TILL YOUR SHOULDERS ACHE
TIL YOUR THIGH MUSCLES CRAMP
TIL YOU CAN'T SEE SHORE
TIL YOU ALMOST CAN'T BREATHE

now maybe you can stop
now maybe you can think

now maybe
you can go home

Coming Of Age

When my father became sixty five
he decided it was time.
This nice old Jewish man
rode the New York city subways
every working day of his life.
He folded his newspaper
in the prescribed manner of all subway riders
once in half
up and down
twice in half across.
That way he stayed in his own space
read his paper
hung on to the overhead strap
while the subway jiggled and swayed
all over the tracks.

He had spent every working day of his life
hunched over
a sewing machine
stitching dresses
his wife could never
afford to buy.
He had thought only about making
enough money to provide for
      his loving wife
      his three wonderful sons
      his baby daughter.

This nice old Jewish man
really decided it was time!
He registered at a driving school
got behind the wheel of a car
for the first time in his life and
he learned how to drive
        very erratically
        very badly.

My father drove all around New York City
across the George Washington Bridge
over the industrial flatlands of New Jersey
through Baltimore, Washington DC, Richmond, Virginia
straight down highway 95 to Florida.
When he got to Miami Beach he found many
unattached
lonely
blue haired ladies
all eager for his company.

He chauffeured these ladies
to senior citizen meetings,
doctor's and beautician's appointments,
to lunch in cafeterias
that were really social centers.
My father tootled that little old car
all around Miami Beach and
up and down the east coast
for the next fifteen years.

II

When I became sixty five
I took my just turned twenty one year old
granddaughter, Wendy
on a trip to Mexico.
We stayed in the Grand Hotel in Mexico City
in a room with twelve foot high ceilings
overlooking the Zocalo.
The hotel had a gold and glass elevator.

We rode up and down
endlessly examining
      the rococo furniture, and
      the rococo people sitting on
      the rococo furniture in the lobby.

We spent a whole day in Chapultapec park
watching the pandas and
walking the corridors of
Museo de Anthropologica.
We religiously visited art museums
The Fine Arts
The Tamayo
The Museum of Modern Art.
We toured the ancient exotic sites of
Teotihuacan
Uxmal
Chichen Itza.

We wore our shoes out shopping the markets
     the thieves market
     the flea market
     the arts and crafts market.
We bargained everywhere and
filled our suitcases to bursting.
We ate in a different four star restaurant each evening
late each evening.

We enjoyed the exquisite cuisine of
Alfredo's
San Angelo's
Los Tres Troubadores.

When we were filled to bursting and our
clothes didn't fit
we took a plane to Acapulco.

We lay flat out on the very white sandy beach.
Swam languidly in the bathtubwarm tropical water.
Roasted in the hot tropical sun.
We slowly recovered from our
     very expensive,
     very enervating,
     very foreign vacation.
Then we flew home and resumed our respective lives.

III

When I become seventy five I'm going to fly straight back
to that beautiful beach in Acapulco.

ALONE

I'll find one of those sloe eyed
silky skinned young beach boys
take his hand
walk him to a hammock
swinging between two palm trees.
The sun will sink slowly into the Pacific ocean
while we drink tequila out of coconuts.
Scruffy little five year old boys
will hawk all manner of strange tidbits
from cazuelas and comals.

We'll buy the juiciest ones and
gobble them up;
ignoring the dangers of
parasites and amoebas.
What harm could come to me in paradise? Such a
            very expensive,
            very enervating,
            very foreign vacation.

I may never go home and resume my respectable life.

Curfew

yes mama, you are right
yes mama, I'll be home by ten
I know, I have to be up at six
I know, I need my sleep
yes mama, I'll be home by ten
I know, I said that last night
yes mama, I'll be home by ten

Andy, Andy, I must get home by ten tonight
Andy, Andy, they'll lock me up forever if I'm late
we'll never have another date
they'll never understand
be sure, be sure, just get me home by ten

what, what, it can't be
let me see
your watch is wrong
I can tell
it's only eight
wait wait
I can't go home

Yet

Condo Pool

Get up early
Strip off nightgown
Pull on swimsuit
Walk five hundred yards
Across the green
Past the gazebo
To the pool.

I own it all
Commons, birds, trees
Not another human being in sight.

What luxury
I don't fill it
I don't filter it
Don't even skim
Just swim
All alone
Only me.

Don't tell the board
If they knew
How important
This is to me
They'd raise
My condo fee.

Now it's only
Half as good

George decided
Since I love it
He'd come too!

Now
Every morning
There are two people
In the pool.

Sh-Sh
Don't tell
Keep it secret
Three people
Would be
Just too much.

Grandpa Berek

Alter Berek strong and tall
Pretended to an education
He never had.

Left a wife and four small children
In Lodz to survive
Somehow
While he went
To seek his
Fortune in America.

Came back after two years
Without the fortune
Tickled the two younger children
Apprenticed the two older children to
A tailor and a dressmaker
To learn a trade
Alter was too proud
To learn a trade.

Left again to seek his
Fortune in America
One year later
Wife and family followed.

How did they ever get the money for passage.
Who helped?

Alter Berek tall and strong
Brought his family to
Three small dark rooms
Up three wooden flights of steps
With a toilet in the hall
Shared by three other families.

Every morning Alter dressed carefully
In the one suit he owned
Put on a clean shirt his wife
Painstakingly pressed
Knotted his only tie
Combed his hair and beard
Arranged his yarmulke on top of his head
Left the house carrying a clean empty
Sack over his left shoulder.

He walked up and down the tenement streets calling
I cash clothes!! I cash clothes!!
Occasionally a housewife came down a stoop
And sold him, for a few pennies,
Clothes she no longer needed
These he sold to a dealer in second hand clothes.

From such foolishness
He thought he could make a living?
Too proud
To learn a trade
Who bought the children's shoes?
How did they pay rent?
How did they eat?

Mornings

It takes much more of the morning
To get ready for the morning these days

Time was when it was up at
Six and out by seven

Nowadays

Up at nine
Or thereabouts
Get up slowly
Must not fall
Acclimate to new
Upright posture

Morning ablutions
All slower paced
Shower soothes slowly
Hot water
Nices achy joints

Swallow those pills
Cream those heels
Get that powder into all
Those cracks and crevices

Now the battle
to get dressed
Hooks have become smaller
Laces are tanglier
Button holes are tighter
And shirts are always inside out.

Finally
All done
Oh my God
It's noon
And no breakfast yet.

Oh well
Let's do lunch

Moving

I never loved that house
we bought it
because we could afford it
and we needed a place to live.

Tall and narrow
one room wide
four stories
from full basement
to full attic.

Small rooms
lots of cubbyholes
a place for everything
and nothing
ever in its place.

Did I leave the hammer in the basement?
no
I last used it in the attic
not   there
search and search and search
finally we find it
in the trunk of the car.

I never loved that house
and now it was time
to leave
it took only thirty five years
to decide
the house was not suitable.

We sold it to a real estate agent
we sold it
as is
so we wouldn't have the hassle
of people traipsing through
examining our lives
and we'd never know
who replaced us
in the little old house.

A friend came to help
with the trauma
of the final packing.

He said he truly loved
two things in that old house
the handworn oak balustrade
and the small stained glass window.

Would we mind
if he had them moved
to his place
and replaced with
some ordinary modern equivalents.

The realtor wouldn't give a hoot
after all he got a bargain
we had sold the house *as is.*

He was a good friend
hard to refuse him
but finally I said,

That would hurt the house
wasn't it bad enough
we were leaving
we couldn't do anything more
to hurt the old house
that we never loved.

Papa

Why did you make me cry?
In front of Josie
My best friend.
She's mean
She'll tease me tomorrow.
When she comes round
She'll make fun of me.

Why did you make me cry?
What I did wasn't so bad
It really didn't hurt the baby—
Too much
She likes to bounce.
Mama wouldn't yell like that
She knows I'm really good.

Why did you make me cry
So hard
After I told you
I'd never do it again.
I'll make you sorry too.
I'll drop dead tonight.

When you see me all dressed
In my Sunday best
In my coffin
Covered with flowers.
Then you'll be sorry.
Then you'll cry.

Tomorrow when Josie comes round
She'll tell me
How you cried and cried and cried.

My Big Toe

If I had any pride at all
I'd never wear sandals
I'd cover my ugly age worn
feet with socks
and shoes

you'd never see
the big right toe's
black and ingrown nail
hurt thirty years ago
when George dropped
a crowbar on it

you'd never see
the second toe on
each foot
stick its second joint
up in the air
like Quasimodo's
bent back

I don't know how
it just happened

you'd never see
all the jagged
chipped nails
almost can't bend
to cut them
when I finally do
they've become too hard
they are
rhino horns

I don't know how
it just happened

one day they were smooth and soft
suddenly for no reason
they became
splintery and striated

If I had any pride at all
I'd never wear sandals
I'd cover my feet with socks
but then you could
read the same story in
my hands
my neck
my unlifted face

Perfect

Not this one
Too hard
No
Not that one
Too soft

This one
This one

Just ripe
Drippy
Sweet
Sour
Tart

The
Perfect
Nectarine

Permanent Employment

We got married
He went to work
I kept house, shopped and cooked
That was my job

We had a baby
He went to work
I took care of the baby
Kept house, shopped and cooked
That was my job

The baby became a child
He went to work
I went to work
Took care of the child
Kept house, shopped and cooked
That was my job

The child left home
He went to work
I went to work
I attended school
kept house, shopped and cooked
That was my job

He retired
I retired
I keep house, shop and cook
Is that still my job?

Bube and Zeyde

Bube Basha made shabbas dinner
For all the children and grandchildren
The daughters helped
The daughter-in-law brought the babka
But Bube Basha worked so hard
Oy, did she get a headache.

Every Friday night
Bube Basha tied a cold wet cloth around her head
"Sh, sha," she said,
"Oy do I have a headache."

Zeyde Alter said, "Come children"
"We'll play."
Zeyde took all the grandchildren
Into the back bedroom
"Let's play, A Bird Flies"
We giggled, we cried
We crowed with glee
"Sh sha"
"Such a headache has Bube Basha."

"Put one finger on my knee
When I say 'a bird flies'
Let your finger fly
Mine will too
When I say,
'A goose flies'
Let your finger fly
But if I say,
'A house flies'
Don't you dare pick up a finger."

Each of us solemnly put one finger on Zeyde's knee.

He said, "A bird flies"
Up went all the fingers
He said, "An airplane flies"
Up went all the fingers
He said, "A butterfly flies"
Up went all the fingers
He said, "A shoe flies"
Up went all the fingers.

Oh how Zeyde howled
How we all yelled and yowled
He caught us
Everyone.

And Bube Basha called
From the kitchen
"Sh, sha,
Oy, do I have a headache."

Homecoming

One

We just had to find a place of our own to live.

It was absolute hell to move back home with my baby,
But there I was and there I stayed for a long year and a half.
I stayed unhappily all the time George was winning the war
By bouncing across France and Germany in a half track.
He was a private with a rifle,
The most expendable soldier in the army.
Would he ever make it back?

He did   He did   He did
He made it back with all his parts intact.
A party   A party   A party
Lots of food, lots of drink, lots of people.
Music, noise, dancing, celebration.
Hearty welcome for the returning hero.

Then came the hard part—
We had to learn to live together.
Being in my parent's house now was purgatory
Not enough space   not enough privacy.
Six big rooms—bedrooms far apart but
Not enough space   not enough privacy.
They could hear us fight, they could hear us make love
And fight again.
Making up was so much harder when I knew they could hear us.
I needed to fight in private
Where I couldn't hear mama in my head.
I needed to fight like a grownup not like mama's little girl.

Oh my God, how we needed a place of our own.
Poor George, five years before he had married
a sweet, compliant seventeen year old with long blond hair
A seventeen year old who was going to school because she did not
know what else to do.
She did know she wanted to get married and have a baby.
Isn't that what every patriotic little girl did
        for the war effort?
And George did what every patriotic young man was supposed to do;
        he married her.
She played house happily.
In due course a year and a half later she had a baby.
But as soon as the baby was born, George went off to fight his war.

Now the hero came home and what did he find?
His sweet compliant little girl was very, very busy.
During the day she worked in a nursery school.
In the evening she took courses toward getting a degree.
She had friends he didn't know and therefore didn't like;
And she would not give them up.
She could take a week off—
        but no more.
She had to work; she would continue at school
She simply could not stay home and play house.
So much for coming home to the gentle joys he remembered.
Even If he wasn't sure he wanted those gentle joys
He certainly hadn't planned on coming home
To somebody else's "had tos", "could nots", and "would nots".

And poor me.
I hardly knew the boy I had married.
But I did know that he had been a sweet and gentle boy,
A talkative City College art major.

Who was this morose man who came back and said he was George?
He sat at the kitchen table and drank Calvados all day.
And he never got drunk.
He barely talked.

We cooked and ate around him.
He barely touched his food.
The level in the Calvados bottles got lower and lower.
The bottles emptied
And he never got drunk.

We seemed to share only one thing, not our child,
Not a remembered
tenderness. but an obsessive need
For a place of our own.
Once we had that, we might begin to talk to each other again.
Once we had that, perhaps we could begin to look
At the fragments of our marriage.
There might yet be something to salvage.
Perhaps together we could find a glimmer of the gentle boy
And the tender girl.
We could go on from there.
We could try.

Two

We found it,   we found it,   we found it.
So what if my mother turned up her nose and said,
"No one lives in railroad flats any more.
The rooms are nothing but one long hallway.
It might as well be one room.
And an icebox! Who has an icebox nowadays?
Who'll carry the ice up? Who'll empty the water?
You'll have a flood every day. Maybe every other day."

"Mama, mama, I won't forget or
  If I do
  I'll mop it, mama
  I'll mop it up."

"The only door is on the bathroom.
And what a bathroom!
A tub with claw feet.

Well, at least the tub's not in the kitchen.
And the toilet's not in the hall. Not shared by neighbors.
But there's no cabinet under the sink.
Copper pipes all exposed.
Sylvie, you'll never be able to polish that copper up.
It's been too neglected. You'll neglect it too."

  "Mama mama
  I don't care
  It doesn't have to shine
  It will be mine
  Not yours
  Mine!"

"The only thing going for this apartment is cross ventilation.
It goes straight through with windows in the front and windows
        In the back.
And what a view! You certainly have a view.
Look out the back and you see the railroad freight yards
        practically in your own backyard.
You really don't have to look out to know the trains are there.
The yard is a switching yard.

You can hear the clanging and the chugging and the tooting
all day long.
All night too.
Want More?
Go up front
Look straight across and you can practically see
into those people's windows.
It's a very narrow street.
They don't even have curtains. Only torn shades.
Look down.
Across the street is where you'll shop.
A candy store. Do you think they really sell candy?
I think they only take bets on the numbers.
I know about such places."

      "I'll never go there
      I promise ,mama
      It'll be all right
      I'll never go there."

"Next to that is a small grocery.
The windows look like they've never been washed.
Don't buy anything but cans in there. You never can tell.
Best of all you can get your religion right across the street.
The two biggest stores are holy roller churches.
They compete to see which one can holler the loudest
And the longest.
You can take your pick.
That is, you can take your pick, if they'll let in white people.
And white Jews at that."

"I never went to schul
I won't go to church
I'll picnic or party
Instead."

"But worst of all are the stairs. Wooden stairs.
Three long flights of wooden stairs.
It doesn't matter that you have to carry every bag of groceries
Up those three long flights of steps.
It doesn't matter that you have to carry all your garbage
And all your laundry down those three long flights of steps.
What matters is that they are WOODEN steps!
They have not built houses like this in I don't know how many years.
They are against the law.
They are against the law because they are firetraps.
I know I know
You say you'll be careful.

What about the neighbor below you?
And the one next door?
What about the house next door?
And the one on the other side?
The houses are all the same.
Narrow stairwells that act like chimneys.
And wooden steps that burn, burn, burn!

Sure there are fire escapes down the front of the building.
And the windows that lead out to them are nailed up tight.
How else do you prevent burglars
        from coming down
Off the roof into your house?

That's against the law too.
Burglars can't get in but you can't get out either."

      "Mama, mama, don't you worry.
       We'll fly up the stairs. We can carry the world.
       We'll fly down the stairs two at a time.
       We'll take the nails out of the window.

       We'll have a place of our own.
       We'll find each other again.
       We'll begin to love our child.
       We'll be safe.
       We'll be warm."

Diet Nightmares

Full pound
Porterhouse steaks
Triple chocolate
Chocolate cakes

And lots and lots of real whipped cream

Two martini
Lunch breaks
New York double
Cream cheese cakes

And lots and lots of real whipped cream

Pâté de foie gras
An elegant paté
Then Haagen Daas
Ice cream-never sorbet

And lots and lots of real whipped cream

An omelet
With lots of cheese
Then just one small
Waffle—if you please

And lots and lots of real whipped cream

Question

I believe what I can see
I believe what I can hear
But sometimes I hear
A voice from so long ago
It couldn't be real.
Mamma says "*Don't do that*"
And I don't do that
Mamma's long gone
How come I hear her?
How come I listen?

This
and
That
and
Much
Such
Important
Stuff

Teaching First Grade

Tell them stories
Read stories to them
Label the door "door"
Label the desk "desk"

Sing alphabet songs
Make up silly rhymes
Like
The cat in the hat chased
The big fat rat

Take trips
Walk to the store
Buy ice cream
Bus to the museum
To see dinosaurs

Admire the pictures they draw
Write what they say
Right under the picture

Somehow
During that short school year
Magic will happen

Children will begin to read
They will
Truly begin to read

Terror

How could she do that
just leave
she's fifteen
he's an ugly
no
a nothing
twenty three

He'll leave her
alone
as soon as it gets rough
alone at fifteen
in the big
cold
evil
frightening world

Who'll take care of her
who will feed her
who will keep her warm
what will they do to her?

I'll close my eyes
and she will come home
I'll go to bed
hide under the covers
and it will all go away

Stay here under covers
dark
warm
see no evil
hear no evil
dark
warm
here under the covers
now
always
forever

That Old House

That old house in the Bronx
Was just 20 feet wide
But it was four stories tall
From basement to attic

I owned the spaces in between
Just ordinary spaces
Like kitchen and bathroom
Bedrooms and living room
Nothing special

George owned the basement
It had a dark room and woodworking bench
He also owned the attic
That was for building ham radios and using them too.

The kids and all their cousins
Dozens of cousins
Begged to be allowed into the cellar and attic
Such interesting smells of sawdust and sparks
Such interesting tools
Like wire strippers and mauls

George would take three or four to the basement
A lucky child would get to hammer in a nail
A luckier one might even drill a hole with a hand held drill
Everyone would get a turn at sanding

Sometimes a whole dozen or so of owl eyed children
would follow George
Up the walnut bannistered steps through the little bedroom
Through the closet door up the narrow attic staircase into
The radio station

There they would cluster round and listen to the
Da-dit magic of Morse code
Then they would talk
Really talk
Sometimes to a ham across town
But sometimes to a ham across the country
Across the ocean

Then they would all troop back down the narrow staircase
Through the closet door down the walnut bannistered staircase
Back out into their own world
Which had just grown
A little wider

Solar Eclipse

July 11th 1991

We gathered friends and neighbors
And neighbors of friends
Up onto the roof patio
On top of our house
In San Miguel Allende

We provided drinks and *antejitos*
We provided Government-approved anti-sun glasses
We provided pin-hole cameras

All of this in preparation
For watching an *almost*
Total eclipse of the sun

For a total eclipse—total darkness
We'd have to travel
To Cabo San Lucas a beach town
On the southernmost spot of
Baja California Mexico
Only 500 kilometers
As the crow flies from San Miguel
But many hours of hard driving
And a long ferry ride
For those of us
Without wings

So we would make do
With *almost*

As we waited for the spectacle to begin
We ate and we drank
We chatted and chattered
We enjoyed the usual brilliant sunny afternoon
We listened to
Burros clomping on the cobbles
Birds chirping and singing
Children shouting and laughing

Then

A breeze began to ruffle the tablecloths
The light changed ever so slightly
And we talked more softly
We looked up
And we could see the tiny moon
Begin to cover
The enormous sun

The wind picked up some
And we chased a few
Wandering hats

No more clattering burros' hooves
Children were quieter
Birds sang more softly

And it wasn't sunny
It was darker
Not dark
Just darker

We looked up
And the tiny moon
Was covering
Half the sun

The wind blew harder
We stopped talking
Even the children were quiet
No bird sang

The wind stopped
We all looked up
The moon was covering almost all the sun

The world stood still
And silent
And the light changed to an
Eerie grey green

Some Days

Some days
the sky is clear and blue
even when it's pouring down rain

Some days
are warm and sunny
even if the thermometer says 10 below

Some days
I soar and fly
even though my feet are mired in mud

Hallelujah
2007

"And the Lord said,
'God helps those
Who help themselves.'"

And way back in 1955
There was a lady
Who helped us all
She was Rosa Parks
She got on a bus
She paid her fare
She sat down in the back
Where Blacks sat
In 1955 in Montgomery Alabama
When white folks filled up
All the front seats and
One white man was left standing
The bus driver said to Rosa
"Git up and stand
So this fella can sit"
And Rosa had had enough
Much more than enough
"No sir, I paid my fare
I'm sittin right where I'm at"
And they put Rosa Parks in jail
And all the black folk in Montgomery
They decided to help themselves
And they would not ride the buses
Until anyone who paid his dime
Could sit anywhere on any old bus

And was it hard
Yes it was hard
Did heads get broke
Yes heads got broke

And people died

And it took a year
A whole hard year
To win that fight
And lawyers worked
In the Supreme Court
Of these United States
So that schools
Were open to all
Politicians worked
To get laws passed
Like the Civil Rights Act
And did that make everything OK
You know it didn't
It took people
Like you and me
risking beatings and batterings
In sit-ins at lunch counters
In freedom rides
In voter registration drives
To get court decisions obeyed
To get the new laws honored

And people died

It took a determined black father
Walking his little girl
Up a long flight of concrete steps
To the white door
Of an all-white school
To show us all
We had more work to do
And brothers and sisters
Look where we are now

One of our best and brightest
Knocked on another white door
The white door of
The White House
And there he is
Working for us all
White and Black alike
And say a Halleluyah for that
      HALLELUYAH

Is there more work to be done
Oh yes there is
But remember where we were
Even back in 1963
When 250,000 folks
Blacks and whites too
Came by bus and train
By plane and on foot

To gather in front of the statue of
Old Abe Lincoln
And listen to the words
Of the great Reverend
Martin Luther King
When he said
"I have a dream
 I have a dream"

If he and Rosa are
Looking down on us now
What do you think they'd say
I think they'd say
We're getting
A little closer to that dream
Oh yes we are
And say a Halleluyah for that
        HALLELUYAH

Is there still work to be done
Oh yes there is
So let's all get up off our butts
And get to work
And say one more Halleluyah for that
        HALLELUYAH

Late Again

Late again
I've dithered and dathered
I've blithered and blathered
And
I'm late again

If I said
I'd never
Ever
Do it again

Would you believe me?
I guess not
That's just a lot
Of silly rot

Oh well, better late than never

Return

He came back to San Miguel
For twenty years he'd held onto the memory of a quaint hill town
Burros meandering up and down rough cobbled streets
Small brown people quietly offering exquisite embroidery for
Approval and purchase
Slow easy pace of a town that had been there for centuries
And would always remain just as it was

     He couldn't stand
     the stink of traffic
     the clutter of shops
     the shoving and pushing of so many people

But worst of all
The geography had changed
The distance from the *jardin* to the *biblioteca*
Had grown much farther
Each hill
And there were more of them
Had grown longer and steeper

     He went back to New York City
     there he could stand
     the stink of traffic
     the clutter of shops
     the pushing and shoving of so many people

Four Eyes

I was seven when I got my first pair of eyeglasses
Kids called me four eyes
Grabbed my glasses and ran away
Teased and taunted
with nary a whit of shame

Do you think I cared?
Not a bit
Not a whit
I could see!
I could read
I learned to protect my precious extra two eyes
I had the whole world to see

Then I grew up
Really old
Like fifteen
Even sixteen

Then did I care
Then did I worry
I looked so much prettier without
The extra two eyes
And I knew!
Dorothy Parker said it
"Men never make passes at girls who wear glasses"
And I knew!
Boys didn't like to dance with four eyes
Only two

I asked Doctor Opto
"Would anything bad happen to me
If I just didn't wear my glasses
On special occasions
Like parties and
Dances?"

"No" said he
Grinning and sighing sadly
"Nothing will happen to your eyes
But when you cross the street
And get hit by a car—"

Sooo
Only on special occasions
When I had a special safe escort
Like George
Did I take off my glasses
Let the world blur
While I whirled and twirled
Flew with the music
Made believe I looked and leaped
Like Ann Miller

That Saturday night
We went to Greenwich Village
To a Ball
To raise money for the
Spanish Republican Army

Dim lights   Loud music
Two bands   Nonstop dancing
Whirling twirling jitterbugging

Flat Foot Floozie
And *Take the A Train*

Glasses safely hidden in purse
Needed to powder my nose
Told George to wait right there
So I could find him!

Came back
No George
Waited
And waited
No George

He asked me to dance
Dancing is better than waiting
We danced one, two, three dances
He was tall
He looked good
He danced almost as well as George
Still no George

He asked me to go for a walk
Not too far
Visit a friend
An Artist
Who lived in the Village
Still no George

I went

We walked three, four, five long Village blocks
Turned one or two corners
Didn't know where we were

Couldn't read the street signs
We climbed a crumbly concrete stoop
Pushed open a creaky door
Tried a doorbell that didn't work
Started up three long flights of wooden steps

We finally reached the top
He called
"Hey, Barto, let us in, let us in!"

A door opened
A one legged black man in BVDs
Hopped out, grabbed him like a
Beloved brother
Pulled him into the room

I followed

The room had a large work table
Covered in paints and canvases
A large bed
And that's all
Nothing more would fit

The walls and ceiling were covered in
A blur of paintings
That I couldn't really see
We sat on the bed
Where else?
He began talking about the artist's
Unique use of color
His convoluted compositions

I reached into my purse
Stuck my glasses on my nose
And WOW!
The room glowed
Vibrated
I relaxed
Forgot how terrified I had been
Just absorbed the light and the glory
The ugly little room disappeared

He who looked good said
"Come, time to go
Barto needs his sleep
You need to get home"

When we reached the street
He turned me around to face him
Roughly
"Why did you come with me?" he asked
        "I don't know,
            I really don't know"
"Don't you ever, ever," he yelled
"Do a crazy fool thing like that again
 Do you know what could have happened?
 Do you know what almost did happen?

 Come on, don't cry
 Little one don't cry
 Nothing did happen

I'll take you home."

Oh My Goodness

Oh my goodness
Beat the drums
Let the trumpets blare
This old girl's
Going somewhere
I jumped down
From the shelf
I'm taking a break
It's an innocent plunge
It's not a mistake

I'm off on a tear
I'm going somewhere
I've got a ride
I've planned the route
Reserved a room
Bought tickets to boot

Ashland, Ashland
Here I come
Blow the trumpet
Beat the drum
Shakespeare's the prize
Just can't fake it
Never ever thought
I'd make it!

Times They Are A-Changing

When I was six I raced cars on every street corner
I thought I knew the risks
But it was such a wonderful high to win
       To wait until the last possible second
       Race across
       Feel the wind of the car
       Whoosh behind me
My only fear—Someone might tell my mother.

When I was fourteen I knew I could save the world
       I walked picket lines
       Any picket lines
       I made speeches standing on a soapbox
       On Union Square
       Telling out-of-work men
       How capitalism had done them in
       Such nice men
       They didn't laugh at me.

When I was an older adolescent still saving the world
       Hormones interfered
       Took chances with all sort of young men
       Some not so young
       Anyone I chose had to be wonderful
       No dangers, I was invulnerable
       Went walking at night in
            Greenwich Village
            Harlem
       No dangers, I was invulnerable.

When I was in the middling years
    There was no time for taking risks
        Make a family
        Raise a family
        Start a career
        Push ahead in it
    Rich, rewarding, busy, busy
    Donate more money than time to good causes
    Protest the war in Vietnam
    But not hard enough to get arrested
    Energy focused on home and husband
    Job and offspring
    Not much left for anything else.

Now in twilight time
    Children are grown
    Career laid aside
    Nestlings have flown
    The time that I have
    Is simply my own
    I can run
    I can fly
    High as I dare
    No one to question
    How why or where

Accomplishment

So I can....
I wrote all day
I revised all night
I tweaked and I polished

So I can....
it is acceptable
it is a competent job
it will fly

BUT

it's not my style
it's not my rhythm
it's not my voice

I won't do it again
not ever, ever
EVER

Bessie Smith

There are very few things I'm too young for these days
But I'm too young to have really heard Bessie Smith
Yet I hear the echoes of her voice
The echoes of her style
Every time I hear a good blues singer
Every time I hear a good jazz singer
Every time a good singer gets
Downright low and sexy

Diagnostics

New university doctor
Suggests, suggests strongly
That I have a colonoscopy
After all colon cancer is second only to
Breast cancer as a killer of women

Stripped down to socks
Given only a skimpy back opened gown
To cover my vulnerability
Led to an empty cubicle
In a long corridor of cubicles

Most cubicles hold a patient on a gurney
Either a *before* or *after* patient
Space is both holding tank
And recovery room
They bring a gurney into my cubicle
Tell me to climb onto it and wait

Wait I did
Chilly, exposed and terrified
For two long hours
Occasionally someone says—
The doctor is running a little late

An IV is shoved into my arm
By a—harried couldn't care less—nurse

I am given the usual papers to sign
Absolving doctors, hospital and the world
For any permanent damage they might
        inflict upon me.

Eventually my good-looking young doctor
        shows up with a cavalier
I'm sorry I kept you waiting—
He then proceeds to declaim each horrifying Word
        on the document of absolution
I had already signed

They wheel me into a soundproof room
Anesthesia and procedure
Begin simultaneously
Stop, I yell, that hurts
No, says doctor, calmly, it won't hurt much
The anesthesia will take hold

The anesthesia does not take hold
He keeps going upward and onward
While I   Howl   Scream
Grovel   Beg   Implore
Try to climb off the gurney

It's all right, he says
It's almost over

It is never over
It is not all right
Sure I'll never have colon cancer
That guy just scraped my colon right
        out of my body
With a rusty kitchen knife

Back in the recovery room
Still on the gurney
Still in socks and back aired gown
I ask WHY WHY WHY didn't you just stop
The dear cavalier says,
Well it sometimes happens this way
Then it is best just to go on
You'll probably never have this procedure
        again.

Damn right
I'll never have this procedure again

I'd die first!

I Don't Belong

I don't belong in most poetry classes
Most poets are serious
I'm usually not

Most poets deal with their innermost feelings
I usually deal with what's for lunch

I don't belong in memoir classes
Most memoirists tell their whole life story
I only want to tell the funny parts

I don't belong in the senior residence
Where I live
Most residents here love bingo

I only play serious intellectual games
Like slot machines

I Hate Rehab

I have to get up early
long before I'm ready
I hate rehab

I walk 2.3 miles
And I never get anywhere
But I'm not so tired

I bike3.1 miles
And I go nowhere
I hate rehab

I climb five flights of stairs
And I'm still on the same floor
But I'm beginning to feel stronger

I do 25 leg lifts
And nothing gets lifted
I hate rehab

I'm beginning to feel better
But I hate rehab
I'm beginning to feel better
But I hate rehab
And better
better
Better!

Inexplicable Magic

He reads from the piece of paper he holds in his hand
The child hearing the tale
Is transported across many seas to a time
Hundreds of years ago
To a land that never was
Where genies come out of tall vases
And children travel the skies
On magic carpets

She looks down at the piece of paper she holds in her hand
The paper has a whole series of
Five parallel lines on it
Scattered seemingly at random
On these lines are strange symbols
Most of them discs with tails
And a few other squiggles
She examines the symbols carefully
Opens her mouth
And sounds come forth
So beautiful
They can only have been made in heaven

He studies the sketch on the piece of paper he holds in his hand
The airship he has drawn
Is beautiful enough to honor a museum's walls
But more than that
When draftsmen have delineated
And engineers have elaborated it
Into actuality
That airship will take man farther than ever before
To new worlds
To other galaxies.

Nestling

Yesterday
Puff ball
Yellow belly
Chick like
Wobbly flight
Open mouthed squawk
Wanting to be fed

Today
Smooth sailing
Wobbly landing
Can't scratch and
Hang onto perch
Squawk becomes song
Almost

Tomorrow
Soaring flight
Steady landing
Sensational song

Mechanics

Told everyone I wrote on the computer
Really thought I did

Didn't count the scribbles on the backs
    of discarded computer paper
         used up good-for-nothing pages of
misspellings, jumbled thoughts, bad writing

Didn't count the mulled up nighttime thoughts
    fragments—half words
        hazy ideas—weird rhymes
that came together in the scribbles

Worked at writing directly on the computer

Sat and stared at the screen for days and
    bleary nights and
        bottom sprung days and
nothing happened

NOTHING HAPPENED!!

Broken Bones

I always knew broken bones don't hurt
Look at skiers in casts and crutches
      smiling up at the camera
Look at little kids grinning while friends
      sign their casts.

Then one day I foolishly stepped up onto a
      three legged stool
And down I came
Banging knee and head and arm, but bad
The knee hurt, the head hurt
But the arm was something different
It raged and howled in a pain that was
Foreign to anything I had ever experienced.

I couldn't understand it
Broken bones don't hurt
Then finally I realized
It would hurt until it was cast
Then it would be all better.

That arm was x-rayed, cast and put in a sling
And it continued to hurt like hell
No way to get in and out of bed without help
No way to get comfortable once I got there
I used a dozen pillows to prop the offending arm
To try to find a position
That didn't ache and ache.

Someone else should take that arm
Till it got better
I sure was doing a lousy job.

It was hard to eat with the wrong hand
But I managed that somehow
Think of the weird sensation of wiping your bottom
With the wrong hand
And what fun it is to try to wash decently
With one hand out of commission.

What were those skiers smiling about?
Why were those kids grinning?

Boobs Breasts and Titties

I was slow
All my friends grew titties long before I did
When mine finally showed up
They were little lemons
Not the melons I had hoped for.

And they stayed that way
I wore a bra
Just so I could wear a bra
Sure didn't need one.

Got married
Became pregnant in a hurry
And I blossomed
My breasts bloomed
So did my belly.

The day the baby was born
My belly flattened flat
But my breasts remained proud and bursting.

The purse mouthed nurse came to my bed
And showed me how to
Wash the big brown nipples before she
Brought the baby in to suckle
"Prepare them both," she said
"And be sure nothing touches them
Once they're ready."

I was a good girl
Did exactly as she asked
Stripped down to my waist
Long blond hair brushed down my back
Tenderly washed my boobs
Sat cross legged on the bed
In all my glory
And waited.

Stiff starched nurse came in
Carrying my bundled baby
Took one look at me
"Cover up girl!" she ordered
"You are making a spectacle of yourself!"

She was exactly right
Just then I was a spectacle
And I loved every minute.

But What Is Poetry Anyway

It's a succinct way of saying something important
   a shortcut way of telling a story
   a lyrical way of expressing an emotion
   a potent way of sharing sadness
It's a lover's way of offering his heart
   a lover's cry when lovers part
   a child's rhyme when she jumps rope
   a burdened soul who cannot cope
   mourners wails when there's no hope
It's a mountaineer's yodel at the rising sun
   a gourmand's satisfaction when a good meal's done
   a skier's joy at a snow covered slope
   a surfer's wahoo when he catches that wave
It's Tiger Woods when he makes a great save
It's the monumental first sight of El Capitan
It's your yahoo at your first grand slam
   a child's elation at his first home run
   a scholar's exalting when his treatise is done
It's a soldier's last breath when death won't wait
It's his mother's howl when she learns his fate
It's the glow of a garden in early Spring
   the sudden quiet when no birds sing
   the cinnamon aroma of just baked apple pie
   the rosy glow of the morning sky
   the camper's sadness at the trip's last hour
   that camper's relief at her first hot shower

It's a six hundred year old sonnet by Shakespeare
       a six year old playing with rhyme
       a three year old beating out time
       the Bard's haunting picture of mad King Lear
It's young ones first glow in young love's glory
It's either Browning telling their story
       the condensed wisdom of a good haiku
       the old family stories that always seem new
It's Merwin sharing Hawaii at its worst and its best
       Hawaii the home of Lindbergh's last rest
It's the scent of a flower
       making love in a bower
       getting drenched in a shower
       looking down from a tower
       feeling that power

That's poetry
That's what poetry is anyway

Go Right

He said "go right"
I said "go south"

He said "go north"
I said "go left"

We fought
We raged
I thought
I'd leave
Forever

But how could I?
We were in the
Middle of Holland
Hunting a museum

That we never found

Hummingbirds

Feeder glued to kitchen window
Elbows glued to counter
Barely morning
Coffee cup in hand
Nose barely a foot from feeder
Tiny fat brown hummer
Beak as long as body
Comes to feed
Settles in for the long pull
Nurses--Suckles
Comes up for air
Flicks translucent tongue
Like a cat licking whiskers
Takes off in a whirring of wings.

Love
and
Loss

A Beginning

So he forgot his wallet
And we drove back 100 miles to get it
He insisted he couldn't go on without it
It could happen to anyone
Couldn't it

So he couldn't find his keys
Well, he couldn't find his keys
About once a week
Even when he was forty

So he can't find his wallet or his keys
Almost every time he leaves the house
And he becomes angry
Really furious
when we are stuck in traffic
That's frightening

So we sit down to a leisurely breakfast
Look out at the chattering sparrows
Feeding at the wondrous feeder he built
His fork slips from his arthritic fingers
He becomes enraged
Actually manic
Bangs his hands against his head

That's fiercely frightening

Progression

Wallet's missing, long miles we drove back
Wallet's found, what happened to the keys
Same story each day just different degrees
Happens to us all, just give him some slack

A vacation trip, yet the road is blocked
He shouts, bangs the wheel, just cannot wait
He rails at the gods and curses his fate
So he gets angry, I shouldn't be shocked

His eyes are puzzled, what day is today
He can't remember, what did you say
What is the name of our daughter's new play
And when did our neighbor move away

I know where it's going, I'm losing you
Our contacts are fading, our friends are few
Forgetting the old, not learning the new
Soon he'll forget to remember me too

Best Friends

Dinah and I were best friends
We played after school
Dressed our dolls and
Combed each other's hair

Wore my mamma's clothes
Put on her jewelry and powder
We knew we would be
Best friends forever

Then Miranda moved in downstairs
She had a Shirley Temple doll
You could comb its hair
That doll even had ice skates

Miranda wanted to be my best friend
I told her I couldn't
Dinah and I were best friends
Forever

Next day
Dinah came and said
You and I can't play anymore
Miranda and I are best friends now

I hit her
What else could I do
But she still wouldn't be
My best friend

That Bridge

I cannot cross
That bridge
My way is blocked
By towering ridge
Of past remembrances

I could easily smudge
Out the pain of being discarded
Just once

I would not bear a grudge
Over an affair that happened
Just once

Only an innocent would return
To sure experience
Of more pain
This seasoned one
Will not oblige
By coming back
Again

Cradle of the Night

Yesterday I lay asleep
In the cradle of the night
And you were there beside me
Just as you were
Before we both were twenty
Tender as a new born lamb
Gentle as our baby's breath
I woke in the morning
And you weren't there
Gone just as you were before
Gone before we both were twenty

Denouement

three little maids from school are we
super friends—great buddies
all from across the tracks
junior high school 101
East Harlem

yet we all made the grade
took the test
scored with the best
now in Hunter College High School
super friends—great buddies
for four long years
no mean achievement at fourteen
when everything changes in two seconds

poodle skirts GREAT
NAH
out of date

Bing Crosby to DIE for
NAH
but Frank Sinatra
AHH

Such a motley crew we three

Katy Greek Orthodox
        tight short cap of
                curly dark hair
                        hard and muscular

Clara the Catholic
        silky black hair
                down to her waist
                        lithe and long

Sylvie the Jew
        dirty blonde hair
                many pounds overweight
                        always

meet every morning
110th street station
Lexington avenue local
ride to 96th street
walk three long blocks
chattering all the way

three little girls
together all day
in each class
so much to plan
so much to talk about

we'd go to the same college
    take the same courses
          teach in the same school
             always together
what could change that?

and Monday
we'd play hooky together
that's how bad we could be
to see Frankie
at the Paramount

no—not Monday
we'll go Tuesday
Monday we have French
and Miss Manay our teacher
is so beautiful in
high heels and silk stockings
not black cotton and low oxfords
like Miss Calvin
our Latin teacher

OK settled
Monday we enjoy French
Tuesday we enjoy Frankie
"and Wednesday" says Clara
"our Latin class goes to my church on 98th
to read Latin prayer books
and that's funny
cause I know Miss Calvin isn't Catholic"

"so what" says Katy
"Miss Manay speaks French and she's Jewish"
"no, she's not Jewish" counters Clara
"she and her mother
take communion at my church"

"Oh goody goody" glows Katy
"she's not Jewish
then I can really like her"

December

Discard, clear away
Remove the dust of our lives
Get rid of old theatre programs
Amadeus, Gielgud in many a Shakespeare play
Night Must Fall—oh yes it must
What need have I for the smiling Buddha
Florida's shells and Guatemala's weavings
Give away our collection of Mexico's treasures
That was another time, another life
All I need are the memories
And I have those
Those I have.

He hoards each yellowed scrap
Broken telephones—broken
Power supplies powering nothing
A crumbling used up water color palette—crumbling
Photograph of a smiling young woman
But who is she—who, who, who
The bike with worn out gears—worn out
An obsolete computer—obsolete
He can fix that broken chair with screws and glue—fix it
He can save the pillow, seal it tight, so nothing oozes out
It's not quite the same now, but still, it gives much comfort.

Dirge

Mourn
Mourn
Mourn
Rend garments
Tear hair

In pain
Bear a son
Nurse a babe
Nurture a child
Raise a man

Sudden death
Time out of joint
Nature awry

Rail at the gods
Rant at the fates
Curse the heavens

And then

Only other living child
Anointed first born son
Dead
Destroyed
Deceased

Howl
Howl
Howl
Life's chain broken

Chalice emptied

Heart Attack

Heart attack at fifty   Almost lost him
But he made it   He made it

Followed orders   Low fat   Low salt diet
Except for Chinese food   Corned beef sandwiches and
Southern fried chicken

Never exercised   Said he couldn't
They didn't mean him anyway

Became the earliest old geezer computer nerd
Computer nerds in the seventies were smooth cheeked children

Soon moving became   Like swimming under water
Hardly able to breathe   Less and less able to breathe

Bypass surgery   Touch and go
But he made it   He made it

Buried in computers   Teaching and learning
Learning and teaching
Then suddenly Prostate cancer   Radiation misery
On its heels   Throat cancer   Radiation misery

Again moving became   Like swimming under water
Not able to breathe   Not at all able to breathe

Emergency bypass surgery   Successful   Heart doing fine
But a stroke   A stroke   As part of the cost

Lost half his vision
Half of whatever mobility he had left
Lost eye hand coordination
Lost   Lost   Lost

Struggles to find words   Struggles to read
Some humor left   Not much
Anger at anything   Anger at nothing   Raging fury

Then lung cancer
Devouring fury
No respite
He died
He died

Heshie

He was born challenging the world
And asking questions

When he was two and a half
His daily allowance, like his big brother's
Was two cents to spend any way
He wished at the corner candy store
He asked for his two cents
As soon as he awakened
In the morning and spent it
As soon as he was allowed to
After breakfast

He was only two and
So he napped every afternoon
When he wakened
He asked mama
For his two cents
Mama explained carefully
He would get his next two cents
When he wakened tomorrow
Blessed Heshie said
"So I slept
So ain't it today is tomorrow?"

At five mom sent him
Off to kindergarten
He came home at noon and said
"I ain't goin there   They don't learn
They just play
I know how to play"

Mama was a hard taskmaster
She said "You go!"
Hesh went
Every day
Came home just like he should
Every day at noon
Then one day after a couple of months
He came home at eleven

Mom asked "Why?"
Hesh responded
"Everybody came home now
So I did too"
Next morning Mom and
Hesh went to kindergarten

Hesh hadn't been in that classroom
Since the first day
He had stayed in the far end of the
Schoolyard and played
When the other kids went home
So did he
Hesh played at home
The rest of that year

First grade was different
Hesh knew he had to go
But such a trial it was
He had to sit still for such a long time
But he swallowed reading
Read everything he could find
Writing was different

His straight lines
Weren't straight   His circles
Weren't round enough

One day the principal came by
And rapped his knuckles
Cause his circles weren't round enough
Hesh bolted
Mom went to school and said "Don't you ever
Ever
Rap my boy again"

No evil deed goes unrewarded
That principal became
Superintendent of schools
For all of New York City

That's how schools were
You were rewarded for silence
Round circles
And vomiting what you'd just been told
Precisely as it was told
Questions weren't asked for
Questions weren't welcomed

Schools weren't ready for Hesh
Life wasn't ready for Hesh
Rest in peace dear Heshie
Rest in peace

Langston Hughes Did It

Langston Hughes did it

Take some Mississippi mud
Make a man
One who'll dance all night
Show a girl a good time

Take more Mississippi mud
Make a man
One who is kind and tender
Who knows when to come home

Mix em both up
Toss and twirl
Til they are just one
Toss in some more

A little bit of the guy
Who puts bread on the table
Likes his kids
Absolutely adores me

Now I've got me a man!

Leo

This phone call made it
From New York City to a
Small mountain town in Mexico
3000 miles away

"My father
Your brother Leo
Had a stroke
Come"

Another call made it
From New York City to
A suburban California town
3000 miles away

"My father
Your brother Leo
Had a stroke
Come"

Brother Seymour and I tried
To meet at Kennedy
We needed to help each other
We needed to hold each other
Up

We searched
We hunted
We called on the PA system
We never found each other

We met finally in the cold
Grey hospital hallway
Where the rest of the family stood
Swollen eyed and weary

My turn to visit
Intensive alien care
This was not Leo
Lying mute and motionless

Leo is the runner
The careful steward
Of his body
The conservator of family

Now alien forces breathe for him
Nourish him
Measure him
Withdraw waste

Where is Leo
Not here
Surely
Not here

Doctor confirms
What all of us see
No cognition
Only automation

Almost in unison we say
Let it stop let it stop
Leo would hate this
He would hate it

Doctor nods and walks away
We push into a stairwell
So we can vent
Our grief in private
We let him go

We let him go
We let him go
Not really
Leo was gone
Long gone
Before we said
Let him go

November

This morning the sugar bowl is almost empty
Someone put a wet coffee spoon into it
    Not me
    I don't ever do that
    Don't even use sugar in coffee

I'll dump what's left in the bowl
And start fresh

What's under that hard opaque crust?
Haven't been to the bottom of that bowl in years
Maybe never
What's under that hard opaque crust
I don't think I want to look

This is the season
When losses come
Sharp
Frequent
Uninvited

I cannot afford to look
Too deep
I dare not invite
More losses

Games People Play At Twilight

Different
Neither worse
Nor better

Frantic and frenetic is not the pace

Just

Leisurely returns to well-traveled places
Joyous recognition of favorite hideaways
Delights to be savored again and again

Playing is pleasure
Not only finale

Both of us
Winners
Every
Time

Mourning 2

Lift up
That lock of hair
Fallen
O'er mine eye

One
More
Time

Lump

My family doctor finds it during a routine checkup.
I never would have noticed it
I'm not much for self-examination.

"Just a small round lump at five o'clock
 in the lower left quadrant of the left breast" he says
"I don't think it's anything, but you had better
 let the surgeon have a look
 just in case."

I go home and find that lump.
For two weeks I poke that left quadrant until it's sore.
I wait for the lump to get smaller, to go away.
It does not get smaller
It does not go away.
I make an appointment with the surgeon for five o'clock.

"My guess is that it is just
 a benign fatty tumor" says the surgeon,
"But we'd better take it out
 just in case."

Whoa, doctors whoa.
I'm not ready
I have to think
I have responsibilities.
I have a two year old who needs a mama.

If it's benign, there's no reason to risk surgery.
If it's cancerous, it's related to the lumps
Under my arm last month.
It has metastasized.

Metastasize, such an ugly word
Unwanted intruders, stealing blood, muscle and organs I need to survive.

If it's benign, surgery is an unnecessary risk.
Logically I should not allow the surgery.
If it's cancerous, it will spread like the wildfire it is.
There are no possible benefits.
Only losses.
But how can I ever know?
How can I bear not to know and get on with my life.

The surgery is terrifying.
A doctor whose eyes smile while the rest of his face remains
mute under the mask.
What is he smiling about? This is anything but funny.
A nurse, who dries my forehead, pats my hand.
"Don't worry dearie, everything is fine" she says.

If everything is fine, why am I strapped to a cold white table
with bright lights blinding me.
If everything is fine,
why are they getting ready to cut into my flesh with sharp knives
searching for malignant evil?

Waking up is tortuous.
I hurt
I hurt
I didn't hurt before.
My left side is tightly bandaged from my shoulder to my waist.
What did they do?
What did they cut away?

How will I know?
How will I ever know?

Many Marriages

A marriage this long
Is many marriages
Or it never could have lasted

First, the hot constant need to touch.   To devour.   Moving apart just to experience the glory of coming together.   To totally absorb.   Holding, letting go, holding again, never sated, never enough. More, more, more!

Then the parting, cruel and wrenching,   compelled by war.   Three long years of growing—not together—but apart.   Their only contact letters without truth....

Letters to her say,
"The countryside is beautiful, all is well."
All is not well for an infantryman in a field in France, six days after D-Day?
Just pure distilled horror.   He finds some solace in shared
injuries and agonies.

Letters to him say,
"The baby is beautiful, all is well."
All is not well for a nineteen year old trapped by the demands of motherhood, daughterhood and no womanhood.
Alone.   Alone with her baby.   Alone with her parents.   Alone.

Then coming back together.   Strangers—they do not know each other.
He, morose in remembered pain. She, no longer the compliant little girl.

Struggling to find a place to come together.   Rasping, raging, hate filled battles.   Each trying to find something to salvage in a relationship between an unrelated he and a non-relating she.

Raising the children.   Some accommodations must be made for the children.   We must meet their needs for love, for succor, for shoes and socks.

Then the professions.   Learning and earning.   Striving for prestigious professional goals.   Still the hungry mouths of children.   Aging parents, failing and needy, his and mine, mine and his.   All mixed up in one huge bubbling cauldron.

A marriage?   No time to wonder, is this a marriage.   Is it working?
Just do what you must and get on with it.   Introspection is a luxury for less frantic times.

Aging parents die
Maturing children leave
Professional demands
Dwindle—disappear

They

are

left

with

just

each

other.

Marriage Gown

I've worn this garment now for many a year
This scar here came early on when
He wrapped himself close in the quilt
And boylike slept deeply
Leaving me shivering
I thought to solve the problem by
Ripping off the gown
Yet never did.

This abraded area occurred
When we couldn't agree
On directions
He said turn left
I said turn right
Anger and tears
Pain and fury
We just went home.

There are pieces missing
Some large some small
They happened each time we thought to move
He said stay
I said go
He said go
I said stay
Throughout a lifetime
So many moves

Colors are changed and faded
How could they not be
So many washings and wanderings
So many turnings and tearings

The gown will still serve
I'll not discard it yet.

Mourning

There is empty space in my bed
Where you rested against me
Like two spoons in a drawer

There's a cold place round my waist
Where your arm warmed me
While I slept

There is no one in the chair beside me
Where you sat
And waited for breakfast

There is a part of my heart
Where you lived
That no longer beats

No matter how fast I run
Or how deep I dig
I cannot fill the emptiness

Leiber Leibe—Beloved Leo

You grew old enough to retire
Spent your winters in San Miguel
We grew old enough to join you.

Every Friday we sang
Friends, relatives and neighbors
Loud and long into the night
All the old songs
The classics—Rock of Ages, Stardust
The folk tunes—John Henry, Kumbaya
The political songs—Drill Ye Tarriers Drill, Kevin Barry.

Then the winter you did not come.
We held tight to the memories
The loud laugh unmistakable in a dark theater
The sharpness of your response in the face of stupidity
The moustache and the Santa Claus beard.
The lifelong commitment to doing good.

We'll still try to sing the songs every Friday night
But who will remember the words
Who will remember all the words.

One Day

Come to me in morning time
Your kisses wet with dew
Come to me at noontide
We'll pledge our love anew
Come to me at twilight
We'll share the setting of the sun
Come to me in darkest night
And two shall be as one

There Are Times

When
      Pain pierces
      With stiletto sharpness
When
      Problems push one
      Into ever deepening
      Thickening quicksand
When
      Answers are
      Unreachable unattainable
      Utterly distant
      Absolutely invisible

Then
      It would seem best
      To burrow
      Beneath the covers
        And
          Just grow
            Smaller
              And smaller
                And smaller

The Orange

He hefts the heavy golden globe.
Takes the long sharp knife and pierces the fruit.
Cuts through the outer pebbly shell.
The knife point enters the core and severs the heart.
Aiyeeeee
I am halved.

The knife cuts quickly and sharply through each half.
The hand picks up one glistening segment.
Both thumbs burrow beneath the hard shell
And macerate the soft flesh.
The greedy mouth comes down
And sucks in the juicy meat.

The hand, the thumbs, the mouth take all.
The hand holds
The thumbs invade
The mouth absorbs
The second, the third, the fourth
All gone
I am done, destroyed.

Nothing, nothing is left
Except
A pungent aroma
That starts to fade
A few drops of moisture
That start to dry up
And some withering husks of shell.

Generation Gap

After she died he retreated into the house
Kept her clothes in the closet
Kept her underwear in the drawers.
He never wanted to come out.

The family gathers for the holidays
The children, the grandchildren, the babies.

We insist
So he comes
But is he really here?

We insist
So he allows it
We thrust a baby at him.
A picture must be taken
A record must be kept.

Red rimmed eyes stare straight into the camera.
Face of many lines.
Lines of age   lines of loss.
Doesn't look at the child he holds so awkwardly.

The child seems ready to burst out
Eager to taste the world.
He reaches forth with face and hands and feet.
He cannot be contained in that circle of old arms.
The child is really here.

Gone

I helped launch that boat
Out into the wide wide sea
When I could no longer see it
I cried
I howled
I beat his chest
"Don't cry" daddy soothed
"I'll make you another boat"
"I'll buy you more lollipops"

I was inconsolable
I wanted THAT boat
I wanted THAT lollipop sailor
The one I could no longer see
The one launched
Into the limitless sea
For the first time
I realized
That something
Someone
Could really
Be gone forever
Immutably
Irretrievably
Gone forever

Requiem

lean against
plant your feet
press your spine against
the hard gray Catskill rock wall

sharp
jagged

remember
conjure up
recall

the soft feel of me
arms creeping up
breasts
pressing against
moving against
hardening against
the hard feel of you

taut
expectant
leaning against
pressed against
becoming part of
the hard gray Catskill rock wall
spiny
splintery

now tell me it doesn't matter
that was then
this is now

let the soft spray of the waterfall
diamonds cascading
droplets catching color
drip slowly into the center of your palm
rivulets
little pools

remember
conjure up
recall
the soft spray of the waterfall
cool
and sweet
as you kissed the center of my palm
inhaled
drank

that first time
tenderly
lovingly

now tell me you don't care
what was then
is not now

lie down beneath the lilac tree
heavy
with bloom
look up through the purpled green light
smell
the perfume

remember
conjure up
recall

that purpled green light
undressing us
caressing us
dappling us both when first we met
drowning
in each other
beneath the blooming lilac tree

now tell me you are leaving
what was then
that is now

When It Comes

It has been fun
A merry tour
Much longer than
I'd ever dreamt

Travelled by car
Chugged by train
Sailed on a boat
Bounced on a plane
Heeled in a helicopter
Glided in a glider
Never a driver
Always a rider

And now
The ride's just about done
Wish me swift passage
It has truly been fun

The Walk

And I walked abroad in a shower of all my days
And you walked next to me
And we talked of what will be
And what had gone before

And a wind whirled the thoughts inside my head
Love me, love me
Want me, want me
Hold me

And we walked abroad in a shower of all our days
And the birds sang only for us
And violets bloomed out of season
Only for us

And day turned into night
And still you walked beside me
And we talked not at all
We just walked

And a wind whirled inside our heads
Love me, love me
Want me, want me
Hold me

Ablutions

Remember
When the thought of a good sized walk in
Shower seemed like pure luxury

When all I had was a shower pouring into a tub
But I could fill that tub with hot water
And lots of suds

I'd slide slowly in
Luxuriate in bubble and steam
Until the bubbles burst
And the water cooled

Then I'd climb happily out of tub
Until next time

Now I have that good sized walk in shower
And I use it a lot
But I do miss the long soaks

I also have the tub
I could still slide in slowly
But
How in the hell
Would I ever get out
DAMN

Listen

Don't be in such a hurry!
Never mind what the ads say.
Listen to yourself.

Are you really having that much trouble?
Can you enjoy a concert or a play
only losing a few bars or phrases?
Everyone loses a few phrases
especially in those British mysteries.

Hearing aids are a pain.
You have to work really hard to
make them work for you.
Sounds don't sound the same
with a plug in your ear,
or two plugs in two ears.
Sounds sound better when
you manage on your own.

Learn to maneuver
so you can lip read.
Buy front row center theater seats.
Get a little closer
so you can lip read better.
Get a little closer
so you can get a little closer.

If this works
GREAT!

But....
If your favorite word is, "WHAT?"
If your favorite phrase is
"Please repeat that."
If your significant other says,
"You just can't make the TV any louder—"

If your next door neighbor
offered to give you the down payment
on another apartment.
Any other apartment
not next door to his.

The time has come.
You really do need an assist.
So get one.

Don't be in such a hurry!
Try more than one.
Take your time in choosing.
Get the hearing aids that suit you best.

They probably cost more than you planned.
Things always cost more than you planned.
You are worth every C note.
Get the very best you can possibly afford.

You're in for some surprises.
Cars, refrigerators and
some of your best friends
will suddenly sound too loud.
Using a telephone may be positively weird.

But what a discovery.
I'd forgotten the richness of the music I love.
I didn't remember that humming birds hum.
I can hear a brook babble, taffeta rustle,
babies crying, eggs frying

and a million other sounds
I thought I had lost forever.

Resentment

I hate it when people tell me to slow down and take it easy
I'll have all of eternity to slow down and take it easy
After I'm dead

I hate it when I've had to give up things like

Long sight-seeing trips
Cause it takes me too many weeks to recuperate when
I come back

Or

Late night cocktails and rich dinners starting well past midnight
Cause my gut rebels and I pay for it with misery
For more than a day

Or

Long hot sexy nights that last till well past breakfast
Cause I no longer have anyone to share them
Not much fun alone

So

I'll keep taking short trips and reading and writing
As long and as fast as I can and want to
As long as I live I want to LIVE

And

When it's done
I hope the God
I don't believe in
Grants me
Swift passage

Say Amen

Bridges Left Uncrossed

I

I cannot cross
That bridge
My way is blocked
By towering ridge
Of past remembrances

I could easily smudge
Out the pain of being discarded
Just once

I would not bear a grudge
Over an affair that happened
Just once

Only an innocent would return
To sure experience
Of more pain

This seasoned one
Will not oblige
By coming back
Again

II

Span beneath them
More than man can measure
Beneath lies a history
Too deep to fathom
Betwixt them stretches an abyss
Filled with failed encounters
Paved with promises unkept
Bespattered with beginnings
That remain
Beginnings

So Many People

In the morning
I walked with grandpa Chiam
We visited grandma Gussie's grave
Then I walked with Chiam through
Row upon row upon row
Of grave stones
And each had a name
Its own name

"Such a shame"
Said Chiam
"So many people
And all of them dead
It's not right
Just not right"

Trouble

Ordinary Double Bed

Space   Between $\longleftrightarrow$ Us   Becomes

Mount Everest   Unclimbable

Amazon Jungle   Impenetrable

Arctic Ocean   Uncrossable

Gobi Desert   Impassible

Diane

It would have been enough to call you friend
You were such a good friend
But you wrapped yourself around me
In my time of need

You took me out of
My mess of misery
And drove me
On long stretches of flat
Soothing highway
To lunch in most elegant
Expensive restaurants
Topped off
By 99 cent
Banana splits
At Dairy Queen

When I needed to cry
You let me cry
Brought me tissues
And diet coke

You never said
"It will get better"
We both knew it wouldn't
It would just end

When it ended
You held my hand
Taught me to work again
Helped me remember
How to laugh

Oh God How I Miss You

About the Author

      Sylvia Berek Rosenthal was born in New York City and spent her salaried working life as an educator, teaching nursery school up through a Master's program in Guidance at Teacher's College Columbia ,University. With the help of her advisor, Professor Edmund Gordon, she initiated a cooperative program between Teacher's College and an East Harlem school district for the training of incipient elementary school guidance counselors. She also worked with Lillian Weber and Deborah Meiers to support open education classrooms in various Manhattan public schools.

      After retiring she spent her working life as a writer. Early on, she wrote personal essays which appeared in various publications in San Miguel and San Antonio. In 2011 she gathered a small group of these relating to food and published them as "Mrs. Letsaveit"

      In 1997 when she was 74, Sylvia discovered poetry and has worked hard at it ever since. A member of San Miguel PEN and San Antonio Poets, she is now involved in writing and poetry groups in the San Francisco Bay Area. This book is an eclectic selection from that work. Sylvia says when she grows up in poetry, she may choose a genre. Right now she explores it all.

www.ingramcontent.com/pod-product-compliance
Lightning Source LLC
Chambersburg PA
CBHW080701110426
42739CB00034B/3357

* 9 7 8 0 9 8 8 3 0 0 6 6 8 *